THE NBA

A HISTORY OF HOOPS

Published by Creative Education
P.O. Box 227, Mankato, Minnesota 56002
Creative Education is an imprint of The Creative Company
www.thecreativecompany.us

Design and production by Christine Vanderbeek
Art direction by Rita Marshall

Printed by Corporate Graphics in the United States of America

Photographs by Corbis (Steve Lipofsky), Dreamstime (Munktcu),
Getty Images (Andrew D. Bernstein/NBAE, Nathaniel S. Butler/NBAE,
Gary Cralle, Tim DeFrisco, Ned Dishman/NBAE, George Gojkovich,
Ron Hoskins/NBAE, Heinz Kluetmeier/Sports Illustrated, AJ Mast,
Fernando Medina/NBAE, Layne Murdoch/NBAE, NBA Photos/NBAE,
SM/AIUEO), iStockphoto (Brandon Laufenberg)

Library of Congress Cataloging-in-Publication Data
Silverman, Steve.
The story of the Indiana Pacers / by Steve Silverman.
p. cm. — (The NBA: a history of hoops)
Includes index.
Summary: The history of the Indiana Pacers professional basketball
team from its start in 1967 to today, spotlighting the franchise's
greatest players and reliving its most dramatic moments.
ISBN 978-1-58341-946-5
1. Indiana Pacers (Basketball team)—History—Juvenile literature. I. Title. II. Series.
GV885.52.I53S55 2010   796.323'640977252—dc22   2009035030

CPSIA: 120109 PO1093

First Edition
2 4 6 8 9 7 5 3 1

Page 3: Center Roy Hibbert
Pages 4–5: Conseco Fieldhouse

THE STORY OF THE

INDIANA PACERS

STEVE SILVERMAN

CREATIVE EDUCATION

CONTENTS

SPECIAL NOTICE

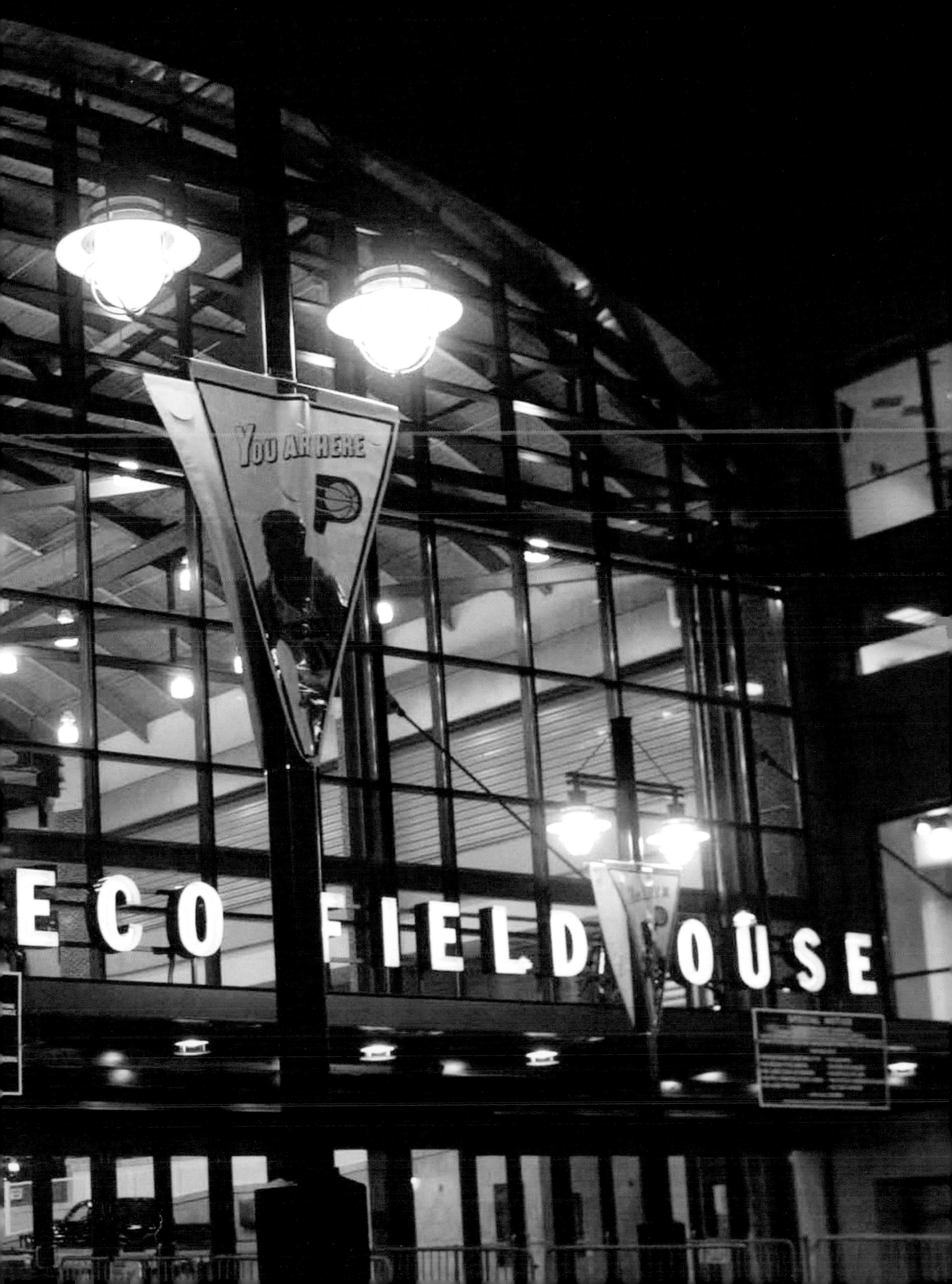
YOU AR HERE
ECO FIELD OUSE

CHAPTER ONE

GOOD TIMES IN THE ABA

"Home of the Hoosiers." It's a title that Indiana residents say with pride, and not just those who attend Indiana University in Bloomington. When many Americans think of the United States' Midwest, they think of Indiana and citizens who are friendly, down-to-earth … and captivated by basketball. Indiana provided the setting for one of the most popular basketball movies of all time. *Hoosiers*, released in 1986, chronicled the run of a tiny high-school basketball team that ultimately defeated a big-city team to capture an improbable Indiana state championship.

Situated in the center of Indiana, Indianapolis is home to two big-time professional sports teams—basketball's Pacers and football's Colts.

ndiana had long been in love with basketball by the time the American Basketball Association (ABA) came into existence in 1967. That league was formed to compete with the stronger and well-established National Basketball Association (NBA), and one of its original teams was placed in Indianapolis. The franchise hit the court bearing a name, "Pacers," that actually had its roots in a different sport—auto racing, in reference to the state's famous Indianapolis 500 race.

Most owners and coaches in the NBA looked at the ABA as more of a curiosity than a legitimate rival, doubtful that the new league would be able to succeed financially or draw big-time talent. It quickly became evident, though, that the Pacers were destined for success, as they swiftly built a solid organization and strong fan base. When the Pacers took the floor for the first time on October 14, 1967, versus the Kentucky Colonels, an overflow crowd at the Indiana State Fair Coliseum watched Indiana come away with a 117–95 victory.

ROGER BROWN WAS ONE OF THE ABA'S SIGNATURE PLAYERS AS THE LEAGUE FOUGHT FOR RESPECT IN THE SHADOW OF THE LARGER NBA. His slashing offensive style became the standard that many great players in later years would emulate, yet if a defender backed off Brown a couple of steps to neutralize his quickness, he would simply drain the outside shot. Brown's pro career never would have gotten off the ground if not for the ABA. As a high-school player, he had been introduced to a known gambler. Even though there was no evidence Brown committed any wrongdoing, the association alone cost him dearly, as he was banned from playing college ball and shunned by the NBA. Welcomed by Indiana, he played on all three of the Pacers' ABA championship squads, was the franchise's all-time leading scorer among ABA players, and was a unanimous selection to the ABA's All-Time Team, as announced in 1997. "He was simply a great player as well as a great scorer," said Hall of Fame forward Rick Barry. "Roger could always make a big play when the game was on the line."

THE ABA WAS A LEAGUE THAT
FEATURED NUMEROUS ELITE
SCORERS. Outstanding defensive
players were a rarity, especially in the
low post. But superb defensive play
helped center Mel Daniels earn the
ABA's Most Valuable Player (MVP)
award in 1969 and 1971, and his
intimidating ability to block shots was
a key ingredient in the Pacers' three
league championships in 1970, 1972,
and 1973. This was never more the
case than in Game 5 of the 1972
ABA Finals between the Pacers and
the New York Nets. With the series
tied at two wins apiece, the Nets held
the lead in the fourth quarter before
Daniels changed the momentum with
one play. New York star forward Rick
Barry went in for what appeared to be
an easy layup. But Daniels blocked
Barry's shot into the hands of Pacers
guard Freddie Lewis, who headed
downcourt. Daniels likewise raced
down the floor, took a return pass,
dunked the ball while getting fouled,
and made a free throw for a three-point
play that propelled the Pacers toward
a crucial 100–99 win. Two days later,
Indiana won Game 6 and the ABA title.

INTRODUCING...

MEL DANIELS

POSITION CENTER
HEIGHT 6-FOOT-9
PACERS SEASONS 1968–74

The Pacers were a competitive team in the ABA that first season but not a dominant one. Yet, under head coach Larry Staverman, the Pacers drew more fans than any other team in the league. Indiana finished with a 38–40 record, and although it made the playoffs, it was swept out of the first round by the Pittsburgh Pipers, who were led by high-scoring forward Connie Hawkins. Such players as quick shooting guard Jimmy Rayl put forth some solid scoring efforts for the young club, but the Pacers needed more talent.

In 1968, the Pacers beefed up their frontcourt by acquiring center Mel Daniels from the Minnesota Muskies. They also made a coaching change, promoting assistant Bobby "Slick" Leonard to the head coaching position. Leonard was a firebrand on the sidelines, a leader whose passion for the game quickly endeared him to the Indiana faithful.

Daniels, along with high-scoring forward Roger Brown and guard Freddie Lewis, gave the 1968–69 Pacers excellent offensive balance, and they assembled a 44–34 record before beating the Colonels in a thrilling seven-game playoff series. In that series, the Colonels built a three-games-to-one lead before the Pacers stormed back to win the last three contests. The Pacers followed that up by beating the Miami Floridians in the Eastern Division finals in five games. However, they fell just short of the league championship, dropping the ABA Finals to the Oakland Oaks in five games.

That loss was only a temporary setback for the Pacers, though. Under Coach Leonard, they dominated the Eastern Division with a 59–25 record in 1969–70. Indiana's greatest strength was its front line of Daniels, Brown, and forward Bob Netolicky. While Brown was a slasher who could either drill jump shots or drive to the rim, the burly Netolicky excelled at holding his ground inside and snaring rebounds alongside Daniels. The Pacers' perimeter play, meanwhile, was led by a pair of guards, sharpshooter John Barnhill and crowd-pleaser Billy Keller.

The Pacers cruised in the 1970 playoffs, sweeping the Carolina Cougars, crushing the Colonels in a five-game Eastern Division finals series, and then capturing the league title by toppling the Los Angeles Stars, four games to two, in the ABA Finals. Brown closed out the Finals in style, netting 45 points in a 111–107 Pacers victory. "Roger was just amazing for us," said Indiana general manager Mike Storen. "[NBA star] Oscar Robertson had told me how good Roger was, and he was even better than I thought he would be. He was a championship player."

CHAMPIONSHIP NUMBER ONE

Bob Netolicky eyes a free throw.

AFTER REACHING THE 1969 ABA FINALS AND LOSING TO THE OAKLAND OAKS, THE PACERS WERE PRIMED FOR A CHAMPIONSHIP RUN IN 1969–70. With center Mel Daniels and forwards Roger Brown and Bob Netolicky leading the way, the Pacers rolled to a 59–25 mark. Daniels was a rugged force in the middle on both offense and defense, but the Pacers' real strength was playing a fast-paced, high-scoring game. The best example of this occurred near the end of the regular season, when Indiana humiliated Pittsburgh, 177–135. In the 1970 playoffs, the Pacers were a runaway train. They defeated Carolina in a four-game sweep in the first round, then routed Kentucky four games to one. There was no stopping the Pacers in the ABA Finals. The Los Angeles Stars had caught fire to advance to the championship series, and they rode the hot shooting of guard Mack Calvin to capture two wins in the series. But Indiana would not be denied. Brown netted 45 points in Game 6 as the Pacers won 111–107 and celebrated championship number one.

CHAPTER TWO

MORE TITLES AND A MOVE

Not content with just one league championship, the Pacers earned a legacy as an ABA dynasty in the seasons that followed, winning two more titles in 1972 and 1973. Indiana claimed its second and third titles due in large part to the 1971 acquisition of superstar forward George McGinnis. Nicknamed "The Baby Bull," McGinnis was a rare physical specimen who combined brute power with smooth moves. "McGinnis is so strong, you'd swear he weighs 300 pounds," said Virginia Squires forward Willie Wise. With McGinnis flexing his muscle, and with superb efforts from such other players as high-jumping forward Darnell Hillman and reliable guard Donnie Freeman, the Pacers beat the Nets in six games to win the 1972 title, then triumphed over the Colonels in seven games for the 1973 championship.

Unfortunately, while the Pacers were cruising (posting winning records again in 1973–74 and 1974–75), the ABA was running out of money. In 1975, the league announced that its ninth season would be its last. Fortunately, the NBA recognized the talent and fan bases of "the other league" and invited

George McGinnis (shown here battling Spurs star George Gervin) ended his Pacers career in 1974–75 with an ABA-best 29.8 points per game.

four of the ABA's best franchises to join. And so, in 1976, the Pacers, Nets, San Antonio Spurs, and Denver Nuggets said farewell to the ABA and hello to the NBA.

Although the NBA offered the Pacers new life, membership did not come without a price. The Pacers and the other three former ABA teams each had to pay the NBA an entry fee of $3.2 million and would not be allowed to share in the league's television revenue for four years—stipulations that made adding new talent nearly impossible. Still, the Pacers persevered, finishing their first NBA season with a 36–46 mark and notching some notable victories. Perhaps most impressively, they beat the defending NBA champion Boston Celtics twice in January, including a 112–101 victory in Boston Garden.

The Pacers got a lift in the late 1970s from the scoring of swingman Billy Knight and the passing of guard Don Buse. Knight could fill up the nets from the outside or penetrate defenses and score inside, and he averaged 26.6 points per game in Indiana's first NBA season. He

THE ABA WAS NOT IN A POSITION OF STRENGTH WHEN THE PACERS, NUGGETS, NETS, AND SPURS WERE ALLOWED TO JOIN THE NBA AT THE START OF THE 1976–77 SEASON. Despite its exciting brand of basketball, the league was hurting for money, and the Pacers were probably in the weakest financial position of any of the teams set to make the merge. Some basketball fans were shocked that the Pacers were selected instead of the Kentucky Colonels, a team that was loaded with stars such as center Artis Gilmore. Many other fans, though, thought that— simply by virtue of dominating the ABA with three league championships— Indiana was deserving of new life in the NBA, star power and financial considerations notwithstanding. "I think when people think of the ABA, they think of the Pacers and the Nets, and I think that had a lot to do with them getting a chance to keep on going," said Julius Erving, a star forward in both the ABA and NBA. "They were such a dominant team. They earned that right to join the NBA."

INTRODUCING...

POSITION FORWARD
HEIGHT 6-FOOT-8
PACERS SEASONS 1971–75, 1979–82

GEORGE McGINNIS

KNOWN AS "BIG MAC" AND "THE BABY BULL," GEORGE McGINNIS PROBABLY GAINED THE MOST FAME PLAYING ALONGSIDE STAR FORWARD JULIUS ERVING AS A MEMBER OF THE PHILA- DELPHIA 76ERS, BUT HE PLAYED HIS BEST AND MOST EFFECTIVE BASKETBALL WITH THE PACERS.

McGinnis was an ABA All-Star in 1973, 1974, and 1975 and was a key contributor on two of the Pacers' three ABA championship teams. A power forward before the term was ever commonly used, McGinnis had incredi- ble physical strength, yet he also displayed the speed and finesse of a much smaller man. He would often call for and get the ball down low, fake to his right, and then attack the basket by spinning left and scoring on an easy layup. Even if opponents knew the move was coming, they often could do little to slow him down. An outstanding football player during his high-school days, McGinnis loved getting physical with his opponents. "I think playing football really helped me," the big forward said. "I like going inside, knocking people around, and coming out with the ball."

SLICK LEONARD WAS ON THE BENCH DURING THE PACERS' RUN TO DOMINANCE IN THE ABA. As an assistant to head coach Larry Staverman in the team's first season, Leonard observed first-hand that many players did not listen to Staverman's instructions. When he was promoted to head coach in 1968, Leonard quickly made clear that he was in command and that his instructions would be heeded. "You got the last guy fired," he told his players, "and I can promise you that you're not going to do that to me." Leonard was a disciplinarian who excelled at firing up his players, and he regularly engaged referees in screaming matches. Leonard's contortions often turned his expensive suits into rumpled, sweat-stained messes, earning him the ironic nickname of "Slick." Not all of Leonard's peers were big fans. Boston Celtics president and general manager Red Auerbach once called Leonard "a dog of a coach." But Leonard got the last laugh by leading the Pacers to three ABA titles. Through 2010, no one had ever coached the Pacers for more seasons than Leonard had.

INTRODUCING...

BOBBY "SLICK" LEONARD

COACH
PACERS SEASONS 1968–80

was quick to share the glory with Buse, who averaged 8.5 assists per game that year and took more pleasure in setting up his teammates with the perfect pass than he did in scoring himself. "It's because of Buse that I'm having a great year," Knight told reporters. "He'll ask me if there's anything special I want to run. I tell him I'll do something, then I do it, and the ball comes right to me." Both Buse and Knight made the 1977 NBA All-Star Game, an achievement that would be the main highlight of the club's first four NBA seasons, as the Pacers posted losing records each year.

Indiana finally broke through in 1980–81, going 44–38 and, under head coach Jack McKinney, making the NBA playoffs for the first time. However, that resurgence was brief, as the team slipped to a 20–62 record in 1982–83 despite the best efforts of forward George Johnson and guard Butch Carter.

Pacers fans had reasons to be optimistic in 1985–86, as Indiana suited up such formidable scorers as center Herb Williams, guard Vern Fleming, and forwards Clark Kellogg and Wayman Tisdale. The Pacers at times appeared capable of putting the ball in the hoop almost at will, but leaky defense undermined their playoff prospects, and Indiana finished at the bottom of the Eastern Conference's Central Division with a 26–56 mark.

CHAPTER THREE

REGGIE ARRIVES

The Pacers' outlook brightened in 1986–87 with the hiring of coach Jack Ramsay. Ramsay, who had led the Portland Trail Blazers to the 1977 NBA title, was known as one of the finest strategists in the league. He excelled at identifying weaknesses in opposing teams that could be exploited and at covering up his own team's flaws by playing "help" defense, in which teammates could suddenly swap defensive assignments in the middle of the action.

Coach Ramsay had some talented players at his disposal in his first season in Indiana. Rookie forward Chuck "The Rifleman" Person provided brilliant outside shooting, Williams and center Steve Stipanovich led the charge in the frontcourt, and Tisdale supplied steady scoring off the bench. Of these players, Person was perhaps most valuable. In his first season out of Auburn University, the forward brought a gunner's

Although he would go on to play for five different NBA teams in all, Chuck Person spent the best six seasons of his career with the Pacers.

mentality to the court and netted an average of 18.8 points per game. Although Person sometimes showed a stubborn and cocky side, Coach Ramsay did all he could to coax the best out of him. Instead of yelling at the talented youngster, the coach employed a calmer, instructive approach. "There are ways to get your point across," Ramsay said. "And mine was never to scream and berate a player. There are plenty of coaches who have done that, and plenty who have failed."

Thanks to Ramsay's guidance and Person's marksmanship, the 1986–87 Pacers went 41–41 to earn a spot in the NBA playoffs for the first time in six years. Although they lost to the Atlanta Hawks, they scored big just weeks later. It was then, in the 1987 NBA Draft, that the Pacers found a player who would be the face of their franchise for years to come: a sweet-shooting guard from the University of California, Los Angeles (UCLA) named Reggie Miller.

Miller was so skinny that some basketball scouts thought he was likely to get seriously injured amid the physical play of the NBA. But while the jug-eared guard was short on bulk, he was long on confidence and talent. Miller had been a big-time scorer at UCLA, earning renown as one of the best three-point shooters ever to play college basketball.

Miller was not dominant in his first NBA season, starting only 1 game and averaging 10 points per game in a reserve role. But his competitive nature was obvious. Miller raced tirelessly around the court, forcing defenders to chase him through screens, and launched scores of deadly outside shots with his remarkably quick release. As Person and Miller blazed away, the 1987–88 Pacers went 38–44.

In 1988–89, the Pacers slipped to 28–54. Although the finish was a disappointment, pieces were falling into place that would make the Pacers a contender again. The team had drafted a 7-foot-4 center from the Netherlands named Rik Smits in 1988, and although his play was initially awkward and at times timid, "The Dunkin' Dutchman" had offensive talent. Indiana had also made a midseason trade to obtain forward Detlef Schrempf, center LaSalle Thompson, and guard Randy Wittman. The Pacers appeared ready to make some noise.

COURTSIDE STORIES

A TASTE OF GLORY

Wayman Tisdale handles the ball during a game in 1987.

THE PACERS STRUGGLED BADLY FOR A DECADE AFTER JOINING THE NBA IN 1976. They were an ineffective and often dull team, and their fans' expectations dropped until Jack Ramsay took over as head coach prior to the 1986–87 season. In training camp that year, Ramsay saw the potential for a big turnaround. Boasting such players as guard John Long, forwards Chuck Person and Wayman Tisdale, and center Herb Williams, the Pacers could fill up the nets. Ramsay's challenge was in convincing players to play unselfishly on offense and with increased ferocity on defense. Some fans worried that Ramsay, at 61 years of age, was too old to relate to his young players. But the coach knew that age was not an issue. "Players want to improve, and they want to win," Ramsay later explained. "They had talent, and we had a plan to get competitive. That's all that mattered, and they played hard." Under the new coach's guidance, the 1986–87 Pacers finished 41–41 and made the NBA playoffs for the first time, earning their first taste of glory in a long while.

CHAPTER FOUR

UP THE CONFERENCE LADDER

nder new coach Dick Versace (who had replaced Ramsay in 1988), Indiana earned a berth in the 1990 playoffs but lost to the Detroit Pistons in the first round. The Pacers then hovered around .500 the next three seasons, making the playoffs each time but losing in the first round every time. In 1993, the Pacers put a proven winner, Larry Brown, on their bench. Brown, a longtime NBA coach, had a rare talent for transforming potential into production. He boasted an uncanny knack for looking at the talent on his roster and figuring out which types of schemes—offensively and defensively—best fit his players.

Center Rik Smits spent his entire 12-year NBA career in Indiana, winning fans over with his loyalty, work ethic, and soft shooting touch.

n 1993–94, Miller and Smits provided most of Indiana's offensive punch. Miller had emerged as one of the most dangerous scorers in the league, while Smits was a major force in the middle, developing a fine hook shot that became nearly unstoppable. Forwards Dale Davis and Derrick McKey, meanwhile, did most of the team's dirty work, hauling in rebounds and battling opposing teams' most physical players. Making valuable contributions coming off the bench, meanwhile, were veteran guard Byron Scott and quick point guard Pooh Richardson.

The new-look Pacers went 47–35 and exorcised their demons by sweeping the Orlando Magic in three straight games in the first round of the playoffs—Indiana's first postseason series victory since joining the NBA. The Pacers then beat the Hawks in round two to advance to the Eastern Conference finals. Although they battled the New York Knicks fiercely for seven games, the Pacers ultimately came up four points shy of reaching the NBA Finals, losing Game 7 by a score of 94–90.

COURTSIDE STORIES

MILLER MAGIC IN THE GARDEN

Reggie Miller in the 1995 playoffs.

REGGIE MILLER HAD A THING ABOUT PLAYING THE KNICKS. After the Pacers had beaten the Magic and the Hawks in the first two rounds of the 1994 NBA playoffs, they squared off against the Knicks in the Eastern Conference finals. The clubs split the first four games before heading to New York's Madison Square Garden. Miller, Indiana's star guard, dropped 39 points on the Knicks in a 93–86 Game 5 win, including a phenomenal 25 in the fourth quarter. Still, New York went on to win the series. A year later, the Pacers met the Knicks in round two of the playoffs, and Miller stole Game 1 for Indiana single-handedly. With 16.4 seconds remaining, Indiana trailed 105–99. Miller then hit a three-point shot, stole New York's inbound pass, and drained another three-pointer. After the Knicks missed two free throws, Miller got the ball, was fouled, and made two free throws to seal an Indiana victory. Six games later, the Pacers won the series. "It was the Hatfields against the McCoys when we played the Knicks," Miller said, referencing the famous historical feud. "It was about doing anything possible to win."

INTRODUCING...

REGGIE MILLER

POSITION GUARD
HEIGHT 6-FOOT-7
PACERS SEASONS 1987–2005

A GOOD ARGUMENT COULD BE MADE THAT, IN THE HISTORY OF THE NBA, THERE HAS NEVER BEEN A BETTER OUTSIDE SHOOTER THAN REGGIE MILLER.

As of 2010, Miller was the NBA's all-time leader in 3-point shots made and had the 13th-highest points total in league history, an amazing achievement considering that Miller was born with deformities in both hips that forced him to wear braces in order to learn to walk correctly. Miller built up his leg strength to compensate for that weakness and developed the devastating ability to shoot the ball in the blink of an eye against bigger and stronger opponents. He was a fearless shooter who was at his best in big games, and he loved the challenge of competing in the playoffs. "I have always thought of myself as a competitor and a fighter," Miller explained upon his retirement in 2005. "I wasn't the biggest, strongest, and I certainly wasn't the fastest. But I wanted the ball in my hands when the game was on the line. I was confident in my abilities, and my teammates were confident in me."

ndiana bounced back admirably from the bitter defeat, charging back to the 1995 playoffs, sweeping the Hawks in the first round, and then exacting revenge on the Knicks in round two by out-dueling New York in another seven-game slugfest. The Pacers once again found themselves on the verge of their first NBA Finals, but they fell apart in the deciding Game 7 of the Eastern Conference finals versus the Magic, losing 105–81.

That loss would stick with the Pacers for several years as the team's upward momentum stalled. In 1999–2000, however, Indiana was back in fighting form. By then, Coach Brown had departed and been replaced by legendary NBA forward Larry Bird. Bird had been one of the greatest players in Indiana history, playing most of his college ball at Indiana State University before becoming a pro star with the Celtics. As a coach, Bird proved adept at conveying his knowledge to his players. As he stressed sound fundamentals and selfless play, the Pacers went 56–26 and were hitting their stride as the 2000 playoffs rolled around.

COURTSIDE STORIES

FLYING WITH BIRD

Coach Larry Bird gives instructions.

MANY GREAT BASKETBALL PLAYERS MAKE LOUSY COACHES. They start running a practice, see that most players can't do things as well as they once did, and give up in frustration. Larry Bird proved an exception to that. The former Celtics great took over as the Pacers' head coach in 1997. Bird demanded discipline from his team and squeezed the most out of such stars as center Rik Smits and guards Reggie Miller and Chris Mullin. Bird had been known for his businesslike approach as a player, and he was just as straightforward as a coach, which endeared him to his players. "Larry treats us like men, and he expects us to act like professionals," Mullin explained after a practice in Bird's first season. "Basketball is not complicated, and Larry doesn't make it that way. All of us appreciate his approach." By the end of the 1997–98 season, the Pacers had posted an outstanding 58–24 record. Bird remained the Pacers' head coach for two more seasons, employing his great strategic and communication skills to lead Indiana all the way to the 2000 NBA Finals.

In the postseason, the Pacers crushed the Milwaukee Bucks and the Philadelphia 76ers to earn a spot in the Eastern Conference finals, where they once again faced the Knicks. Thanks to Miller's clutch play and the versatile efforts of forward Austin Croshere, Indiana topped New York in six games and advanced to the NBA Finals for the first time. There they met a Los Angeles Lakers team that featured star center Shaquille O'Neal and young guard Kobe Bryant. The Pacers managed to win two games—including a 120–87 blowout victory in Game 5—but were eventually overpowered. "It will always hurt," Miller said. "They had a great team, and I'm not disputing that. But to get that close and not win will always be with all of us."

COURTSIDE STORIES

FINALLY, THE FINALS

Austin Croshere scores against the Lakers in the 2000 Finals.

THE PACERS WERE GIVEN LITTLE CHANCE BY BASKETBALL EXPERTS WHEN THEY MET THE LOS ANGELES LAKERS IN THE 2000 NBA FINALS. Los Angeles featured enormous center Shaquille O'Neal at the top of his game, as well as up-and-coming star guard Kobe Bryant. Veteran guard Reggie Miller was Indiana's top weapon, and the Los Angeles native found an extra bit of motivation competing for an NBA championship versus his hometown team. Miller, center Rik Smits, guard Jalen Rose, and the rest of the Pacers lost the first two games of the series in Los Angeles. The Pacers' situation then became dire as the teams split the next two games in Indiana's Conseco Fieldhouse. In Game 5, Indiana played arguably the best game in franchise history, a 120–87 runaway victory. Rose notched 32 points, Miller netted 25, and the Pacers held Bryant to a mere 8 points. "It all came together for us for that one night," Rose said. "It was beautiful." Unfortunately for the Pacers, Game 6 proved to be the end of the line, as the Lakers won the game, 116–111, and the series.

CHAPTER FIVE

THE PACERS RETOOL

The 2000–01 season was one of change for Indiana. Bird stepped down as head coach, Smits retired due to foot ailments, and veteran forward Dale Davis was traded to Portland for young forward Jermaine O'Neal. Miller's backcourt running mate, point guard Mark Jackson, left Indiana as well.

Fortunately, the Pacers found a new star in guard Jalen Rose, who, in his fifth season in Indiana, averaged 20.5 points per game. Behind Miller and Rose, the Pacers won 8 of their last 9 games and made the playoffs for the 11th time in 12 seasons. It was a brief postseason experience, though, as Indiana fell to the 76ers in the first round.

Before the 2001–02 season, the Pacers remade their image via a huge trade in which they sent Rose, guard Travis Best, and a draft choice to the Chicago Bulls for four players, including forwards Ron Artest and Brad Miller. Artest, the focal point of the trade, brought tremendous energy and physicality to the team. At a quick and brawny 6-foot-6, Artest was a

Although he stood 6-foot-8 and was slow afoot, Jalen Rose frequently played point guard due to his great passing and court vision.

skilled offensive player, but he truly excelled on the defensive end of the court. The trade gave Pacers fans a renewed sense of optimism, as Indiana's lineup now featured Miller—a veteran leader who could still knock down clutch shots—playing alongside the quickly improving O'Neal and the fiery Artest.

The Pacers went 48–34 in 2002–03. Then, under new coach Rick Carlisle, they surged to a league-best 61–21 record in 2003–04. Miller credited both Carlisle and better teamwork for the improvement. "It was a good match for our personality and the type of players we had," Miller said of Carlisle's hiring. "Rick really knew his stuff, and he was good at coming up with plays and matchups for us. At the same time, we were working together and making our shots." Unfortunately, that fine season ended in disappointment, as Indiana fought past the Celtics and Miami Heat in the playoffs, only to fall to the Pistons in the Eastern Conference finals.

The Pistons factored into another unfortunate Pacers moment in 2004–05. Tempers were high as the two clubs met in Detroit's arena, The Palace of Auburn Hills, early in the season. After Artest was called

for a hard foul on burly Pistons center Ben Wallace, a Pistons fan hit Artest with a lobbed drink. Artest and such players as Pacers swingman Stephen Jackson charged into the crowd to confront the fan, setting off a wild brawl both on the court and in the stands. The incident put an ugly mark on the NBA's reputation and left Indiana without a key player, as Artest was suspended for the rest of the season.

The Pacers bounced back from that infamous incident to finish 44–38, then defeated the Celtics in seven games in the first round of the playoffs, winning Game 7 in a shocking 97–70 blowout in Boston. Unfortunately, the momentum from that win did not carry over into the next round, as the hated Pistons once again knocked off the Pacers.

Indiana traded Artest to the Sacramento Kings early in the 2005–06 season. The Pacers went 41–41 without him, leaning heavily on

O'Neal—who netted an average of 20.1 points per game—to remain competitive in the Eastern Conference. The Pacers made a quick exit from the 2006 playoffs, then missed the next postseason for the first time in 10 years.

The Pacers then began to sputter, posting 36–46 records in both 2007–08 and 2008–09, then going 32–50 in 2009–10. Miller had retired, and new stars such as high-scoring forward Danny Granger, quick point guard T. J. Ford, and burly center Roy Hibbert stepped up to lead the offense. Although Indiana missed the playoffs for the fourth consecutive year, new coach Jim O'Brien was optimistic. "We think that we have put together some good young players," he said. "There's no reason why we can't take a nice full step forward next year."

Danny Granger was a scoring machine, becoming Indiana's leader—and an NBA star—by netting 25.8 points per game in 2008–09.

JERMAINE O'NEAL CAME INTO HIS OWN AFTER BEING TRADED TO THE PACERS FROM THE TRAIL BLAZERS. The lanky forward had first come into the league in 1996 as a high-school phenom. Noting his size, speed, and athleticism, many NBA scouts predicted stardom for the young man. He never averaged more than 4.5 points per game during 4 seasons with Portland, but he improved steadily once he donned a Pacers jersey. After averaging 12.9 points a night during his first season with Indiana, O'Neal gained confidence and developed an accurate touch around the basket. The 2001–02 season proved to be his breakthrough year. O'Neal led the Pacers in scoring and rebounding and was voted the NBA's Most Improved Player. The honor lit a fire in O'Neal, who was not satisfied with his 19-points-per-game average. "I want to get to the point where I can destroy the entire league," he said upon accepting the award. Unfortunately, a litany of injuries limited his effectiveness starting in 2004–05, and O'Neal was traded to the Toronto Raptors in 2008.

For more than 40 years, the Pacers have been a source of pride in Indiana. From their days as an ABA dynasty to their years as an NBA championship contender behind sharpshooter extraordinaire Reggie Miller, the Pacers have almost always given their faithful fans something to shout about. As Indiana's team continues its quest toward an NBA title, the club in yellow and black plans to set a winning pace again soon.

Pacers fans counted on the scoring of Troy Murphy (below) and slick assists of T. J. Ford (opposite) to help resurrect Indiana as a contender.

INDEX